W9-API-338

DATE DUE

STARGAZERS' GUIDES

Quantum Leaps and Big Bangs!

A History of Astronomy

Andrew Solway

Heinemann Library
Chicago, Illinois

© 2006 Heinemann Library
a division of Reed Elsevier Inc.
Chicago, Illinois

Customer Service 888-454-2279
Visit our website at www.heinemannraintree.com

Design by Richard Parker and Tinstar Design
Illustrations by Jeff Edwards
Printed in China by WKT Company Limited

10 09 08 07 06
10 9 8 7 6 5 4 3 2 1

Library of Congress Cataloging-in-Publication Data
Solway, Andrew.
  Quantum leaps and big bangs: a history of astronomy / Andrew Solway.
    p. cm. -- (Stargazers guides)
  Includes bibliographical references and index.
  ISBN 1-4034-7712-4 (library binding - hardcover) -- ISBN 1-4034-7719-1 (pbk.)
  1. Astronomy--History--Juvenile literature. I. Title. II. Series.
  QB28.S65 2006
  520.9--dc22
                    2005029111

Acknowledgments
The author and publishers are grateful to the following for permission to reproduce copyright material: Alamy p. **7** (Janine Wiedel Photolibrary); Antiquarian Images p. **10**; Copyright 2005 Lynette Cook p. **43**; Corbis pp. **6**, **37** (© Bettmann); Galaxy Picture Library pp. **8** (Robin Scaggel), **18**, **28**; Harcourt Education p. **32** (Tudor Photography); Science Photo Library pp. **5** (Dr Seth Shostak), **11** (Steve Percival), **13**, **15** (David Parker), **16** (Detlev Van Ravenswaay), **17** (Gianni Tortoli), **19**, **20** (Sheila Terry), **22** (D.A. Calvert, Royal Greenwich Observatory), **23**, **24** (Sheila Terry), **25** (John Howard), **26**, **30** (Detlev Van Ravenswaay), **31** (NASA), **29** (Detlev Van Ravenswaay), **33** (National Optical Astronomy Observatories), **34** (Tony & Daphne Hallas), **35** (Emilio Segre Visual Archives/American Institute Of Physics), **36** (Michael Dunning), **38** (John K. Davies), **40** (NASA), **41** (NASA/Jpl), **42**.

Cover image of Big Bang reproduced with permission of the Science Photo Library.

The publishers would like to thank Dr. Geza Gyuk of the Adler Planetarium in Chicago for his assistance in the preparation of this book.

Every effort has been made to contact copyright holders of any material reproduced in this book. Any omissions will be rectified in subsequent printings if notice is given to the publishers.

The paper used to print this book comes from sustainable resources.

Contents

Words appearing in the text in bold, **like this**, are explained in the Glossary.

Sky-Watchers

Astronomy is one of the oldest sciences. To learn about the universe, you have to watch the skies. Today, astronomers use all kinds of equipment to do this. Yet ancient astronomers only had their eyes—and a lot of patience.

Ancient sky-watchers

In ancient times, people used astronomy for several things. Farmers used the skies as a sort of **calendar**. The Sun, the Moon, and the **constellations** (groups of stars) in the sky change through the year. So, farmers would know when to plant their crops by watching for a particular constellation to appear.

Another use for astronomy was to predict the future. For many ancient people, the heavens were where the gods lived. By watching the skies, people thought they could learn about what the gods were doing, and how this might affect the future.

Astronomy was also good for **navigating** (finding your way around). For instance, in the northern hemisphere, if you travel toward the pole star, you are going north.

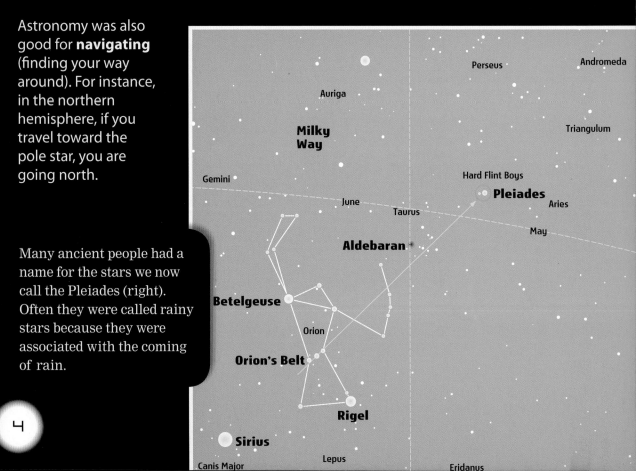

Many ancient people had a name for the stars we now call the Pleiades (right). Often they were called rainy stars because they were associated with the coming of rain.

A quantum leap

Since ancient times, astronomers have made a **quantum leap** in knowledge. Astronomers today can look deep into space. They can send spacecraft on journeys of millions of miles. They have discovered all kinds of incredible things, such as colliding **galaxies** and **black holes**.

This book looks at how we went from sky-watching to space exploration and at some of the great scientists who have helped along the way.

HOT NEWS:
Ancient knowledge

Even before things were written down, people understood how the Sun, the Moon, and the stars moved in the skies. These are some of the facts that ancient people knew:

- The Sun rises in the east each day and sets in the west.
- Outside the tropics, the Sun rises higher in the sky in summer than it does in winter.
- The Moon is full (a bright circle) every 29 or 30 days.
- Between each full Moon, the Moon shrinks to darkness (new Moon) and then grows back to full again.
- The stars are arranged in fixed patterns, called constellations.
- The constellations move across the sky.
- The constellations we can see change position during the year.

Astronomers are now able to use computer technology to control powerful telescopes. They are able to see things that early astronomers did not know existed.

Ancient Astronomers

Probably the very first reason people looked at the sky was to keep track of time. We measure out our lives in days, months, and years. All these units of time are based on movements of Earth, the Sun, and the Moon.

Days, months, and years

The most basic unit of time is the day. Today, we know that day and night happen because Earth spins around once each day. Ancient people measured longer stretches of time by changes in the Moon. The Moon changes from full (a bright disc) to new (black) and back again in just over 29 days. So, people divided time into **lunar months** of 29 or 30 days.

In most parts of the world, there is also a cycle of seasons that happens each year. A complete cycle of the seasons is called a **solar year**. This is the time it takes Earth to go around the Sun once.

The main part of Stonehenge was built over 4,000 years ago.

SCIENCE FACT OR SCIENCE FICTION:
Stonehenge

The stone circles found in many parts of Great Britain, Ireland, and France may have been used for a type of astronomy. For instance, Stonehenge, in England, may have been a sort of calendar. Certain stones marked important times of the year, such as midsummer's day (the longest day of the year). Some people think that Stonehenge may even have been a giant astronomical computer!

Different calendars

To keep track of passing time, people developed calendars, with names or numbers for the months and years. Yet making a calendar that works is not so simple. This is because the cycles of days, months, and years do not fit together easily. A month is not a whole number of days: it is a little more than 29 days. A year is just over 365 days, but this is not a whole number of days or months.

Many early calendars were based on a year of twelve lunar months. This meant that each year was several days short of the solar year, so every so often an extra month had to be added to bring the months and years back in line.

Our modern calendar is based on the solar year, rather than on lunar months. The months do not match up with the cycles of the Moon.

The Chinese New Year, shown being celebrated in this picture, is calculated using the cycles of the Moon.

Your Future in the Stars

For many ancient people, heaven (the sky) was where the gods lived. So, sky-watching was an important part of religion. Many early astronomers were also priests. They watched the skies carefully for signs that the gods were pleased or angry.

Reading the stars

If looking at the sky could tell priests about what the gods were doing, then maybe it held clues to the future. Predicting the future from looking at the stars is known as **astrology**. Priests in the ancient kingdom of **Mesopotamia** in the Middle East were probably the first to use astrology, starting over 3,500 years ago.

Mesopotamian astrologers advised their king or ruler what to do. When there were important decisions to make, such as whether or not to go to war, the ruler would consult with the astrologers. They would tell the ruler whether this was a good or bad time for what he or she was planning.

Astrologers spent much of their time watching the skies, so they were also good astronomers. They used math to try to figure out if there were patterns to the events they saw. They were the first people to predict fairly accurately when lunar **eclipses** would happen. Lunar eclipses are when the shadow of Earth dims the full Moon.

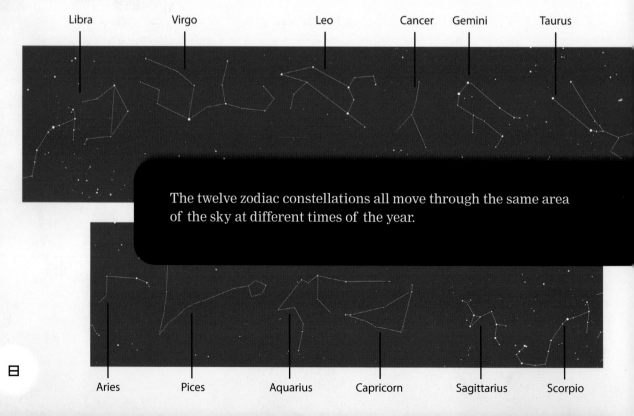

Libra   Virgo   Leo   Cancer   Gemini   Taurus

The twelve zodiac constellations all move through the same area of the sky at different times of the year.

Aries   Pices   Aquarius   Capricorn   Sagittarius   Scorpio

Astrology today

There is no scientific evidence that the stars affect our lives. Yet people still use astrology to predict the future. If you look in most newspapers, you will find a section on horoscopes. These horoscopes are general predictions of what might happen to you. Horoscopes are based on a person's star sign. There are twelve star signs. Each one is a constellation that you can see in the night sky at certain times of the year. Your star sign depends on when you were born. For instance, anyone born between March 21 and April 19 has the star sign Aries (the Ram).

HOW IT WORKS:

The zodiac

The twelve star signs used in horoscopes are known as the signs of the zodiac. They are constellations that appear in skies at particular times of the year. All of them travel through the sky in a path similar to that of the Sun.

Constellation	Name in English	Symbol	Dates
Aries	The Ram		March 21–April 19
Taurus	The Bull		April 20–May 20
Gemini	The Twins		May 21–June 21
Cancer	The Crab		June 22–July 22
Leo	The Lion		July 23–Aug. 22
Virgo	The Virgin		Aug. 23–Sept. 22
Libra	The Balance		Sept. 23–Oct. 23
Scorpio	The Scorpion		Oct. 24–Nov. 21
Sagittarius	The Archer		Nov. 22–Dec. 21
Capricorn	The Goat		Dec. 22–Jan. 19
Aquarius	The Water Bearer		Jan. 20–Feb. 18
Pisces	The Fishes		Feb. 19–March 20

Finding Your Way

Another important use of astronomy for ancient people was for navigation. This was especially important at sea, where there were no landmarks to help ships find their position. Until modern times, sailors used the positions of the Sun, the Moon, and the stars to help them navigate.

Master navigators

The first real master navigators were the Polynesians. Nearly 4,000 years ago, Polynesian people began to spread out from eastern Asia to islands in the Pacific Ocean.

The Pacific is a huge ocean with very little land. To get from one island to another, navigators needed to be very skilled. Polynesian navigators could tell where they were from the angle of the Sun in the sky or the position of different stars above the horizon. They remembered this information and passed it on by putting it into stories.

Polynesian navigators used the Sun and the stars to travel between islands in canoes like this.

TRY IT YOURSELF:

Finding your latitude

If you live in the northern hemisphere, you can find your latitude by measuring the angle between the pole star and the horizon. At the North Pole (latitude 90°), the pole star is overhead at certain times of the year. At the equator (latitude 0°), it is on the horizon.

Another way to find latitude is to measure the angle of the Sun above the horizon at noon. At the equator, the Sun is directly overhead at noon. At the North Pole, it is on the horizon.

Using instruments

In other parts of the world, people took much longer to learn how to navigate using the Sun and stars. Two inventions made it easier for sailors to find their way around. The first was the compass. In the 1100s, the Chinese started using magnetic compasses so that sailors on ocean-going ships could find their way in any weather.

With a compass, sailors could tell which direction they were sailing. Another instrument, called the backstaff, helped navigators measure the angles of the Sun or stars in the sky when at sea. This information is very important for finding your **latitude** (how far you are north or south of the equator). An instrument called the astrolabe had been used to measure these angles since about CE 400, but only on land. The backstaff was first used in about 1600.

The sextant was invented in the 1700s as an improvement on the backstaff. It is still used today for measuring the angle of the Sun, Moon, or stars above the horizon.

Writing Things Down

Many things in astronomy happen slowly. For instance, slight "wobbles" in Earth's axis (the imaginary line it rotates around) affect the positions of stars in the sky over thousands of years. So, it is important for astronomers to keep records to help keep track of these slow changes. The first astronomers to write down what they saw were from ancient China.

Court astronomers

As in Mesopotamia, rulers in China believed that the movements of the stars affected what happened on Earth. So, from the earliest times, Chinese emperors had royal astronomers who watched the skies carefully and wrote down what they saw. For instance, Chinese astronomers were the first to record sunspots (darker spots on the Sun). They also made careful records of solar eclipses (when the Moon hides the Sun), lunar eclipses, **meteor showers**, and **comets**.

HOW IT WORKS:
Chinese astrology

Like the Mesopotamians, the Chinese were interested in astrology. In Chinese astrology, it is the year you are born that is important, not the time of year. Each year is named after one of twelve different animals.

Traditional Chinese year	Modern year	Zodiac animal	Date New Year begins
4691	1993	Rooster	January 23
4692	1994	Dog	February 10
4693	1995	Boar (Pig)	January 31
4694	1996	Rat	February 19
4695	1997	Ox	February 7
4696	1998	Tiger	January 28
4697	1999	Hare/Rabbit	February 16
4698	2000	Dragon	February 5
4699	2001	Snake	January 24
4700	2002	Horse	February 12
4701	2003	Ram/Sheep	February 1
4702	2004	Monkey	January 22

This picture shows the Crab Nebula. It is a huge ring of gas and dust in space. The Crab **Nebula** is the remains of a supernova that Chinese astronomers saw and wrote about in 1054.

Exploding stars

From as early as 100 BCE, there are Chinese records of "new stars" and "guest stars." Today, we think that these records are descriptions of **supernovas**, incredible events in which stars blow up in an enormous explosion.

We think of stars as being unchanging, but astronomers have shown that stars do in fact change over millions of years. Supernovas happen when large stars die. In a supernova, a star may become millions of times brighter for a short time.

When a supernova happens, a star may suddenly "appear" in the sky that was too faint to see before. This is what Chinese astronomers were seeing when they recorded the appearance of "new" stars, which then faded over several weeks or months.

Astronomy in Ancient Greece

Ancient Greece was an important center of learning from about 40 BCE to CE 500. Other early astronomers observed events in the sky and tried to figure out from past events what might happen in the future. Greek astronomers worked in a different way. They were interested in explaining the universe, or at least as much of it as they knew about. They developed models of how the universe might be arranged and then tested them against real observations of the sky.

Models of the universe

One early model of the universe was suggested by an astronomer named Eudoxus, who was born around 390 BCE. He suggested that Earth was the center of the universe, and that it did not move. Surrounding Earth were several different transparent spheres (balls). The Sun, the Moon, and the **planets** were each attached to one of these crystal spheres, and each moved around Earth. On the outside was a final sphere, which was covered in tiny points of light. These were the stars. The great thinker Aristotle, who lived at about the same time as Eudoxus, thought that this model was basically correct, although he suggested a few changes. About 100 years later, an astronomer named Aristarchus suggested that the Sun was at the center of the universe, and that Earth and other planets went around it.

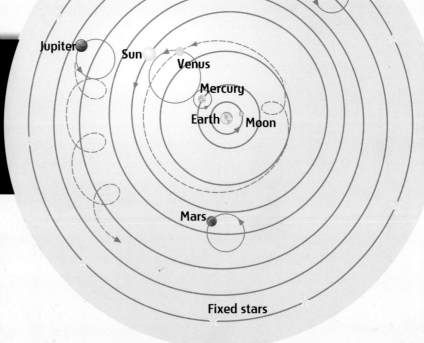

Ptolemy's model of the universe (right), with Earth at the center, was accepted for over 1,000 years after he died.

Making measurements

The ancient Greeks were also interested in taking measurements. The mathematician Eratosthenes agreed with Aristarchus that the world was round, and he figured out a way to measure its size. The answer he got was quite close to modern measurements.

Ptolemy

Ptolemy was a Greek astronomer who lived in Alexandria, Egypt, around CE 100. He brought together most of the ideas of Greek astronomy in a book called the *Almagest*. Ptolemy improved on the Earth-centered ideas of Eudoxus and produced a model of the universe that fitted quite well with observations. Unfortunately, Earth was still at the center of this model, so it was wrong!

Greek astronomers used an instrument called an astrolabe to measure the angles of objects in the sky quite accurately. Arab astronomers improved upon the Greek design. This is an Arab astrolabe made between 1350 and 1450.

Biography:
Arabic astronomers

Between CE 700 and 1200, the Middle East was the most important center for astronomy. Arab astronomers translated the works of the best Greek astronomers into Arabic and improved on many of their measurements. The Persian Omar Khayyam (1048–1131) is best known today as a poet. However, he was also a skilled astronomer. His calculation of the length of a year was the most accurate made until that time: 365.24219858156 days.

Moving the Sun to the Center

In Europe during the **Middle Ages**, Greek ideas about astronomy were accepted as truth. But in the 1400s and 1500s centuries, Europeans began to question the work of Greek thinkers.

Copernicus

One European who read the Greek ideas on astronomy was a Polish astronomer named Nicolaus Copernicus. Like some other astronomers of his time, Copernicus was unhappy with the idea that the Sun, Moon, and planets all circled Earth. This explanation did not agree with measurements and calculations of the actual movements of the Sun and planets. A much better explanation was that all the planets, including Earth, **orbited** (went around) the Sun, while the Moon orbited Earth. But there was a problem . . .

Most pictures of Copernicus are based on a painting he did of himself when he was young.

SCIENCE FACT OR SCIENCE FICTION: Was Copernicus first?

Copernicus is usually described as the first person to suggest the Sun-centered model of the universe. Yet the ancient Greek thinker Aristarchus suggested that the planets went around the Sun nearly 1,800 years before Copernicus. Ancient writings from India also suggest they thought the same thing. However, Copernicus did support his arguments with calculations.

Against religion

In Copernicus's time, the Roman Catholic Church was an important part of people's lives in Europe. Copernicus himself was a canon (a type of priest), and his uncle was a bishop. The Church was strongly in favor of the idea that Earth was at the center of the universe. To go against the views of the Church on this subject was a serious matter. It was almost like going against God.

Publication

Although Copernicus was convinced his ideas were right, he was very nervous about telling other people what he thought. He published a short summary of his ideas in about 1514. Yet it wasn't until 1543 that he actually published a book with all the details of his Sun-centered model.

When the book first came out, it had a "letter to the reader" in the front. This was put in without Copernicus's permission. The letter said that the ideas in the book did not claim to be true, but that they were just a good way to calculate the movements of the Sun, planets, and stars.

In Copernicus's model of the universe, the Sun is at the center and the planets orbit around it. Mercury is closest to the Sun, then Venus, Earth, Mars, Jupiter, and Saturn. Astronomers at the time only knew about six of the nine planets in the solar system.

Laying the Groundwork

Most astronomers disagreed with Copernicus when his book was first published. The Danish astronomer Tycho Brahe was one of those who disagreed with Copernicus. Yet Tycho's own work laid the foundations for a real proof of the Sun-centered theory.

Seeing an eclipse

Tycho became interested in astronomy in 1560, when he was fourteen years old. That year, astronomers predicted an eclipse of the Sun, and the prediction proved to be correct. Tycho saw the eclipse and never forgot it. From then on, he was hooked on astronomy.

From the age of nineteen, Tycho traveled to several universities, learning and collecting instruments to help him observe the skies. Tycho had a hot temper and was always getting into trouble. He got into a sword fight with another student, and his nose was almost cut off. He wore a metal plate on his nose for the rest of his life.

Tycho Brahe (left) was famous for the accuracy of his observations of the stars and planets. His assistant, Johannes Kepler (right), also went on to be a famous astronomer (see pages 20–21).

A new star

In 1572 Tycho made an observation that made him famous among European astronomers. He saw a new star in the constellation of Cassiopeia. The star got brighter night by night until it was brighter than all the other stars and planets. Then, it gradually faded again. He had seen a supernova.

Careful observations

In 1576 Tycho persuaded the king of Denmark to build a new observatory in Denmark. Tycho worked in this observatory for over twenty years. He made the most accurate measurements of the positions of planets and stars before the invention of the telescope.

Tycho's Danish observatory was called Uraniborg. Tycho wanted everything to be the very best quality. As a result, the observatory cost a huge amount to build.

Biography:
Sophie Brahe (1556–1643)

Tycho Brahe had a sister, Sophie, who was ten years younger. Sophie wanted to learn astronomy, but Tycho advised her to avoid subjects that were "too abstract and complicated for the female mind." However, she ignored his advice and taught herself a great deal of astronomy in a short time. After this, Tycho recognized her talent and admitted she was "equal to any man." For a time, she worked as an assistant in Tycho's observatory.

Ovals, Not Circles

In 1599 Tycho Brahe moved to Prague (now in the Czech Republic). Here, he took on a new assistant, a German named Johannes Kepler. Tycho died just two years later, and Kepler took over his job. Unlike Tycho, Kepler was sure that Copernicus's Sun-centered model of the universe was right.

Astronomical tables

Kepler took over the thousands of measurements that Tycho had made during his life. His job was to use the information to create a new set of astronomical tables. These were lists of the positions of the Sun, the Moon, and the planets at different times. Kepler eventually finished the tables in 1627, but he also used Tycho's measurements to try to prove Copernicus's theory.

Kepler's discoveries were very important. They changed the way astronomers studied the movement of the planets forever.

Kepler's laws

When Kepler began to compare the Sun-centered model with Tycho's measurements, he was disappointed. The measurements didn't quite fit. Kepler tried to figure out what was wrong. He worked on just one orbit, the orbit of Mars, for several years. Then, in 1605, he found the answer. The planets did not move in circles—they moved in **elliptical** (oval) orbits. He published his results in 1609.

Proving Copernicus right

Between 1618 and 1621, Kepler published a book explaining Copernicus's theory and his own discoveries. His book provided strong evidence that the Sun-centered model of the universe was right. Astronomers could no longer ignore Copernicus's ideas.

DO IT YOURSELF:
Draw an ellipse

An ellipse is a special kind of oval with two "centers," or focuses. To draw an ellipse, you need a pencil and paper, two stick pins, and a loop of thread. Stick the pins into the paper and put the loop of thread around them. Put the pencil point in the loop, too, then, keeping the thread taut, draw around the pins.

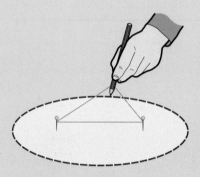

Kepler showed that the planets move in ellipses, not circles. An ellipse is an oval with two imaginary "centers," or focuses. The Sun is at one focus of the ellipse.

Sun at one focus of ellipse

Mars

Imaginary second focus

New Technology, New Ideas

While Kepler was figuring out how the planets moved, a new invention was being developed in the Netherlands. The first telescopes were very simple, with just a lens at each end of a long tube. Yet this simple instrument changed astronomy completely.

Who was first?

No one quite knows who actually invented the telescope. In 1608 three Dutch eyeglass-makers all made simple telescopes and claimed the invention as their own. Within a few months, word of the new invention had spread across Europe.

Galileo's telescopes

In July 1609 the great Italian scientist Galileo heard about the new invention. Within a few months, he had made a telescope that magnified twenty times. This was much better than any other telescopes at the time.

Galileo was the first person to use a telescope to study the heavens. He found that there were mountains on the Moon and figured out roughly how high they were. He also looked at the **Milky Way** (the milky white band of light across the night sky) and discovered that it was made up of millions of stars. Then, he turned his telescope on Jupiter and found that it had four moons orbiting around it. Today, we know that Jupiter has over 60 moons, and many of the other planets have moons, too. Yet Galileo's four moons (Io, Europa, Ganymede, and Callisto) were the first of Jupiter's moons to be discovered.

This is one of Galileo's first telescopes. He ground the lenses for his telescopes himself.

New discoveries

It was not long before other astronomers had telescopes as powerful as Galileo's and were making new discoveries. Astronomers found that the Sun had spots, Jupiter had stripes, and Saturn had rings. People's ideas about the heavens were never going to be the same again.

TRY IT YOURSELF:

Observe the Moon

When Galileo made his first telescope, he began by looking at the Moon. On a clear night when the Moon is full, look at it with a pair of binoculars or a small telescope. You should be able to see darker and lighter patches on the surface. You should also be able to spot some craters—for instance, ones called Tycho, Copernicus, and Kepler. You can see where they are in the photo below.

Copernicus

Kepler

Tycho

Gravity Everywhere

By the 1600s, astronomers had accepted that the universe was a real place, not the home of the gods or crystal spheres. But if the universe was real, how did it work? According to Copernicus, the planets moved around the Sun. But what kept the planets in orbit? And why did they keep moving?

The big attraction

The answers came from one of the greatest scientists of all time, Isaac Newton. Born in England, Newton was a brilliant mathematician, rather than an astronomer. He knew, from the work of Kepler, that planets move faster when they come closer to the Sun and slower as they move away. There had to be a force of attraction that pulls the planets toward the Sun. Newton realized that this force could be **gravity**.

Newton was the first person to realize that the gravity that held things on Earth could also hold planets in their orbits.

Not just on Earth

On Earth, gravity pulls everything down to the ground. Yet Newton had an idea. What if gravity doesn't just work on Earth? What if it is a force that attracts all objects to each other?

Newton proved that gravity really is the force holding the Sun and planets together. Gravity is a force that attracts all objects toward each other. The heavier an object is, the stronger its gravity. The Sun is extremely heavy, so its gravity is very strong. The pull of the Sun's gravity keeps the planets in orbit. Without gravity, they would shoot off into space.

SCIENCE FACT OR SCIENCE FICTION:
Newton and the apple

Everyone has heard the story. Newton was sitting in an orchard one day, thinking about how the universe was held together. As he sat there, an apple fell on his head. "Aha!" he thought, as he came up with the laws of gravity.

This story is probably not true. Still, Newton first came up with his ideas about gravity when he was staying at his family home in Lincolnshire, England. And his family home certainly had an orchard. Who knows?

Newton studied at Cambridge University, in England, from 1661 to 1665. When plague (a fast-spreading, deadly disease) closed the university in 1665, he spent the following two years at his family home in Lincolnshire (shown above). He studied the notebooks he had compiled at school and developed his basic ideas about gravity.

Moving the Planets

Newton did not stop at proving that gravity holds the universe together. He also explained why the planets keep moving endlessly around the Sun. It is because there is nothing to stop them!

Forces and motion

Before Newton was born, the Italian scientist Galileo had done many experiments on how things move. Newton studied Galileo's work and that of other scientists. He came up with three laws of motion that could be used to explain any kind of movement.

Newton's first law of motion was the law that explained what keeps planets moving. This said that if there are no forces (pushes or pulls) on an object that is moving, it will keep moving in a straight line. The planets do not move in a straight line because there is a force on them all the time—the pull of gravity between the Sun and each planet. This force makes the planets move in elliptical orbits. Yet since there is no force actually slowing the planets down, they just keep moving.

Newton's ideas gave astronomers a picture of the solar system similar to the one we have today. However, only six planets were known in Newton's time.

In addition to all his other scientific work, Newton also invented a new kind of telescope. His **reflecting telescope** used a curved and a flat mirror instead of lenses.

Air brakes

On Earth, things do not keep moving in a straight line forever. This is because there are always forces that slow down moving things. For instance, the air around us acts like a brake on things that move through it. In space there is no air, so there is nothing to slow down the planets as they orbit the Sun.

Connecting Earth and heaven

Newton's work showed that the laws of gravity and motion that affect things on Earth have the same effects in space.

TRY IT YOURSELF:
Feeling air resistance

When you are just walking along, it is difficult to notice that air is slowing you down. Yet if you ride fast down a hill on a bicycle, you will feel a strong wind pushing on your face and body. The wind is caused by the air resisting your movement and slowing you down.

Aiming for the Stars

In the 1600s, most astronomers focused on studying the Sun, Moon, and planets. The telescopes of the time were not powerful enough for serious studies of the stars. Yet one astronomer changed all this.

All done with mirrors

When a young man, William Herschel worked as a musician. However, after he moved from Germany to England, he became interested in **optics** (the study of light). Soon, he was using telescopes to look at the night sky.

Herschel realized that he would need a more powerful telescope if he wanted to look at the stars. He built several large reflecting telescopes, making the mirrors himself. His telescopes were among the best in the world.

Looking at the fuzzy patches

Herschel spent over twenty years studying the skies. He was especially interested in nebulas. These are small patches of light that are fuzzy, rather than sharp points like stars. Herschel recorded over 2,500 nebulas. He showed that many of them were actually groups of very distant stars.

William Herschel's sister Caroline was also an excellent astronomer. She worked with William, but also made many observations of her own. She plotted the positions of over 500 new stars.

Herschel showed for the first time just how immensely far apart the stars are and how far away they are from Earth. He was able to figure out roughly how far away nearby stars were and could then estimate the distance of other stars based on their brightness. However, these estimates were inaccurate because Herschel assumed (incorrectly) that all stars have about the same brightness.

A new planet

In March 1781 Herschel saw a "curious star" in the sky. After watching it for several nights, he realized it was not a star, but a new planet. It was Uranus, the seventh planet in the solar system.

HOT NEWS:
Predicting a comet

Comets are balls of ice and rock that travel in huge orbits around the Sun. If a comet gets close to the Sun, it partly melts and develops a long "tail."

The English astronomer Edmond Halley studied a comet that appeared in the sky in 1682. He used Newton's laws to figure out its orbit. From his calculations, Halley predicted that the comet would appear again in 1758. His prediction came true, and the comet is now called Halley's Comet, after him.

Halley's Comet continues to appear every 75 or 76 years. It was last seen in 1986 and will appear again early in 2062.

Unexpected Wobbles

Newton's laws of gravity and motion had made astronomy an exact science. Astronomers could use Newton's laws to predict how objects in space should move. Yet sometimes the laws did not seem to work correctly.

Uranus misbehaves

Herschel's discovery of Uranus caused great excitement, and many astronomers began to plot its movements. Yet as they made more observations, they became puzzled. Uranus was never where it was supposed to be. It was not moving as Newton's laws predicted it should.

One explanation was that Newton's laws were wrong. Yet this was unlikely, since they worked everywhere else. Another explanation was that there was something unknown that was affecting the movement of Uranus. Astronomers realized it could be another planet.

HOT NEWS:
Finding Pluto

In the early 1900s, astronomers began to look for a ninth planet because they noticed small "wobbles" in the movements of Uranus and Neptune. At the Lowell Observatory in Arizona, astronomers built a special telescope and camera to look for the planet. In 1930 a young U.S. astronomer named Clyde Tombaugh found a tiny new planet: Pluto. But the discovery was amazingly lucky, because Pluto was much too small to have affected the orbits of Uranus and Neptune. The "wobbles" that astronomers thought they had seen turned out not to have happened at all.

Pluto is so cold that its surface is made of frozen methane (the gas used in stoves) and carbon dioxide. Pluto has its own moon, Charon.

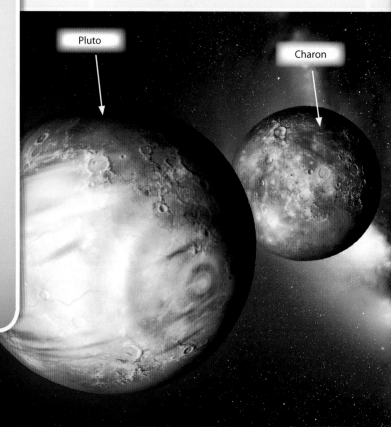

Pluto

Charon

Looking in the right place

In the 1840s, the British astronomer John Adams and the French astronomer Urbain Le Verrier separately calculated where a planet would need to be to make Uranus move the way it did. Astronomers then began searching the sky to see if they could find this planet. In 1846 the German astronomer Johann Galle and his assistant, Heinrich d'Arrest, found a new planet just where it was expected to be. The planet was named Neptune.

The existence of Neptune was predicted before the planet was actually found.

The Colors of the Stars

By the mid-1800s, astronomers had plotted the positions of many thousands of stars. However, they still knew very little about them. Then, astronomers found they could use another of Newton's discoveries to find out just what a star is made of.

Splitting light

In addition to studying gravity and motion, Newton made many studies of light. He showed that a **prism** (a pyramid-shaped piece of glass) can be used to split white light into a rainbow of colors called a **spectrum**.

TRY IT YOURSELF:
Make a spectrum

You can make a spectrum using a flashlight, a jar of water, and a small mirror. Put the mirror at an angle in the jar of water. In a dark room with white walls, shine the flashlight at the mirror. With a bit of experimenting, you should be able to produce a spectrum on the wall.

Lines in the rainbow

In 1814 a German optician named Joseph von Fraunhofer noticed that there were several thin, dark lines in the spectrum of the Sun. For several years, no one could explain this. Then, in the 1850s, two German scientists, Gustav Kirchhoff and Robert Bunsen, made an important discovery. They showed that each chemical **element** produces light of a very specific color when it is heated. Kirchoff and Bunsen then found that the dark lines in the Sun's spectrum are caused by the particular elements it is made of. The lines showed that the Sun is made mostly of the gas hydrogen.

The lines in a spectrum gave astronomers a new way to study the stars. By looking at the spectrum, they could find out which elements were in the star. The spectrum is also affected by the temperature of the star (see page 39).

HOT NEWS:

A new element

In 1868 the French scientist Pierre Janssen found some lines in the Sun's spectrum that did not match up with the lines of any element on Earth. He had found a new element, which he called helium. Soon after it was discovered on the Sun, scientists also found helium on Earth.

This is a spectrum for the star Arcturus. The dark lines in the spectrum are caused by gases in the star's **atmosphere** that are absorbing some of the light.

From Galaxy to Universe

William Herschel was the first astronomer to show that many nebulas in the night sky are actually groups of distant stars. Yet he and later astronomers still had no real idea of the enormous scale of the universe. This was partly because their telescopes were not powerful enough to show very distant stars. Another reason was that many stars within our own galaxy are hidden by clouds of dust.

Galactic arguments

At the beginning of the 1900s, astronomers still did not know just how big the universe was. Many thought that our galaxy was the whole universe. Some astronomers thought the galaxy was disc-shaped, while others thought it was a band of stars.

There were also arguments about some nebulas that had a spiral shape. Some astronomers thought that these were clouds of gas and dust, while others thought they were huge spirals of stars.

The Andromeda galaxy is the closest spiral galaxy to Earth. Edwin Hubble found that it is about 2 million light-years (12 million trillion miles) away from us. It is about 200,000 light-years across, twice as big as our own galaxy.

Other galaxies

The U.S. astronomer Edwin Hubble found the evidence that ended the arguments. From 1919 Hubble worked at Mount Wilson Observatory, in Pasadena, California, which at the time had one of the largest telescopes in the world. Between 1922 and 1924, he looked at several nebulas and was able to show that they contained stars. He also figured out how far away these nebulas were. They were far beyond the stars in the Milky Way (our own galaxy): they were separate galaxies.

SCIENCE FACT OR SCIENCE FICTION: Finding aliens

Today, we know that there are billions of other galaxies besides our own. With so many stars and galaxies in the universe, many people believe that there must be other intelligent beings out there. Yet the universe is so vast, we may never find out about them. For instance, a radio message from Earth would take two million years to get to the Andromeda galaxy!

This picture shows Edwin Hubble using the main telescope at the Palomar Observatory in California.

Big Bang

Once Hubble had shown that there were other galaxies beyond our own, astronomers quickly found many more of them. Not all of these galaxies were spiral-shaped: some were shaped like soccer balls or footballs, while others were irregular.

Hubble began studying the different galaxies and trying to sort them according to their shape. While he was doing this, he made an incredible discovery.

Zooming apart

When he looked at the spectra of the galaxies he was studying, Hubble found that the dark lines in the spectrum (see pages 32–33) were not in their usual places. This was because the galaxies are moving away from Earth. Hubble found that very distant galaxies are moving away faster than those closer to Earth. He realized that the whole universe is expanding!

Astronomers today know a surprising amount about the Big Bang. Much of the knowledge comes from mathematical models of what conditions would have been like during the Big Bang.

In the beginning

Hubble's work suggested that the universe has been expanding at a constant speed for billions of years. How did this happen? A Belgian scientist named Georges LeMaitre suggested that the universe began in an explosion, and that it was expanding as a result of this.

In the 1940s, the Russian-U.S. astronomer George Gamow studied Le Maitre's ideas and improved on them. He called the explosion that started the universe the Big Bang. Today, most astronomers think that the universe suddenly began this way about fifteen billion years ago.

George Gamow (left) was not the first person to suggest that the universe began with a huge explosion, but he figured out many of the details of what happened in the Big Bang.

HOW IT WORKS:
Red shift

How can you tell from the spectrum of a galaxy that it is moving away from you? The answer is something called red shift.

When an ambulance rushes past you on the street, you have probably noticed that the sound of its siren changes. The siren sounds higher as it comes toward you and lower as it goes away.

If something is moving fast enough, the light from it changes in a similar way. If it is moving toward you, the colors become bluer. If it is moving away, the colors are redder. So, if the light from a galaxy is red-shifted, the galaxy is speeding away.

Different Telescopes

The spectrum of visible light runs from red to violet. Yet there is a much bigger spectrum of invisible **radiation** (rays similar to light) that extends beyond either side of the visible spectrum. The invisible spectrum runs from radio waves at the "red" end to X-rays and gamma rays at the "violet" end. In the 1900s, astronomers began to build new telescopes that looked at the skies using these invisible rays.

Radio telescopes

The first new type of telescope was the radio telescope. Astronomers began to use radio telescopes in the 1930s.

Strange new objects were discovered using radio telescopes. In 1961 the U.S. astronomers Thomas Matthews and Allan Sandage discovered that some "stars" produced very powerful radio waves. They called these objects quasars. Quasars are now known to be very distant galaxies that produce incredible amounts of energy.

This is the Carlos Sanchez infrared telescope on Tenerife in the Canary Islands.

X-ray vision

Telescopes that pick up X-rays were first built in the 1970s. They had to be launched into space to work, because Earth's atmosphere absorbs most X-rays from space.

X-rays are very high-energy radiation, so they detect high-energy events. In 1972 the X-ray **satellite** *Uhuru* picked up strong signals from an invisible X-ray source in the constellation Cygnus (the Swan). It was called Cygnus X-1. The signal came from an object orbiting around a massive blue star that was 30 times bigger than the Sun. Cygnus X-1 is smaller than Earth, but its gravity is strong enough to pull gas away from the star. Because it is so small and has such strong gravity, astronomers think that Cygnus X-1 is a black hole.

HOT NEWS:

The first invisible radiation

The first kind of invisible radiation was discovered by William Herschel in 1800. Herschel tested a spectrum with thermometers to see if different colors of light had different temperatures. He found that the temperature of the light increased from blue to red. He then measured the temperature just past the red end of the spectrum and found that it was even higher. Herschel realized that there must be some kind of "invisible" light in this area. We now call it **infrared** radiation.

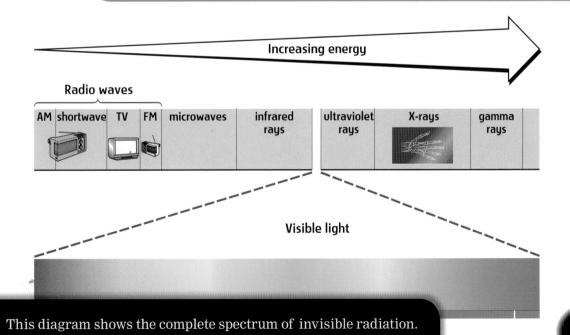

Increasing energy

Radio waves

| AM | shortwave | TV | FM | microwaves | infrared rays | ultraviolet rays | X-rays | gamma rays |

Visible light

This diagram shows the complete spectrum of invisible radiation.

Space Astronomy

Looking at the universe from Earth's surface is like looking through a dirty window. The atmosphere muddies the view and completely blocks some kinds of radiation. So, since the 1960s, astronomers have been sending instruments into space for a better view.

Space observatories

Telescopes in orbit around Earth have enabled astronomers to look even farther into space. Many satellites carry small telescopes and other instruments. There are also a few larger instruments. The Hubble Space Telescope (HST) is a large space telescope that detects mostly visible light. It has been sending back incredible pictures from space since 1993. Other large telescopes include the Chandra X-Ray Telescope and the Spitzer Space Telescope.

HOW IT WORKS:
Evidence of the Big Bang

Soon after the Big Bang, the whole of space was so hot that it glowed. The universe was opaque (you could not see through it). In every direction in space, there is a very small amount of "background radiation" that does not come from stars or galaxies. This background radiation is a faint echo of the burning hot glow of space before there were stars and galaxies.

This map was made by a satellite that mapped the background radiation over the whole of space. The pink areas are slightly warmer and the blue areas are cooler.

The Spirit Rover landed on Mars on January 4, 2004, to photograph the surface of the planet.

Probing the planets

Scientists have also sent unmanned spacecraft (space probes) to explore the solar system. Space probes have visited all the planets except Pluto. Probes have also traveled to comets, meteors, and the Sun. Some space probes fly past planets, taking pictures and sending back information. Others remain in orbit, sometimes for several years. Some space probes carry small landing vehicles that parachute down onto the surface.

New knowledge

Traveling into space has hugely increased our knowledge about the universe. Space probes have shown us volcanoes on Jupiter's moon Io, a lake of methane on Saturn's moon Titan, and close-up pictures of the head of a comet. Telescopes have taken pictures of colliding galaxies and huge gas clouds where stars are born. They have sent back evidence that the Big Bang happened and that black holes exist. New discoveries are being made all the time.

What Does the Future Hold?

Today, we know an incredible amount about the universe. Humans have visited the Moon, and we have sent spacecraft to most planets. We understand how stars are born and die. We even think we know how the universe started. Yet there are still many questions to answer.

Not enough "glue"

One question to answer is why the universe does not fly apart. Gravity is the "glue" that holds the universe together. Yet there has to be enough **matter** ("stuff") for the force of gravity to work.

Recently, astronomers have found that the stars and other objects they can see don't add up to enough matter to hold the universe together. There needs to be about 99 times more "stuff"! Astronomers think there must be huge amounts of dark matter out there, or "stuff" that we cannot see. Finding out about dark matter is a big task for the future.

The James Webb Telescope is scheduled for launch in 2011. It is designed to look farther back in time than the Hubble Telescope, to the time when stars and galaxies formed.

The first stars and galaxies

Astronomers have pieced together quite a lot of information about the early history of the universe. They also know about the universe's history back to about five billion years ago. However, they know very little about the time in between, when the first stars and galaxies formed. Astronomers hope to find out more about this middle part of the universe's history by building more powerful telescopes that can look farther back into the past (see below).

Searching for life

Recently, astronomers have found other stars that have planets circling them. If there are other planets, there may be alien life on them. It is unlikely that we will be able to travel to these planets in the near future. Yet one day we may be able to build telescopes powerful enough to clearly see them and to look for evidence of life.

HOW IT WORKS:
Seeing into the past

When we look at, say, the Andromeda galaxy through a telescope, we are not seeing the galaxy as it is today. Andromeda is so far from Earth that its light takes about two million years to reach us. So, as we look farther into space, we are also looking farther back in time.

Star GJ876 has two large, Jupiter-like planets orbiting it. Between them is a smaller, rocky planet, which could be like Earth.

Astronomy Timeline

about 3000 BCE	Earliest written materials on astronomy from China, Egypt, and Mesopotamia.
about 2900 BCE	Building of Stonehenge begins.
about 2000 BCE	The earliest calendars drawn up in Egypt and Mesopotamia.
about 2000 BCE	Polynesians begin to use stars for navigation at sea.
about 1300 BCE	Oldest record of an eclipse of the Sun (from China).
about 350 BCE	Eudoxus suggests his Earth-centered model of the universe. His ideas are supported by Aristotle.
about 280 BCE	Aristarchus suggests that Earth revolves about the Sun (Sun-centered model of the universe).
about 240 BCE	Eratosthenes measures the circumference of Earth with great accuracy.
about CE 150	Ptolemy writes his famous work, the *Almagest*.
800s to 1100s CE	Arabic and Persian astronomers draw up star charts and catalogs, make better calculations of the length of a year, and translate Greek astronomical writings.

1054	Chinese astronomers observe a supernova in the constellation Taurus. The remains of this explosion are known today as the Crab Nebula.
1543	Copernicus publishes his model of a Sun-centered universe.
1572	Tycho Brahe discovers a supernova in the constellation Cassiopeia.
1576	Brahe builds his observatory at Uraniborg.
1582	Pope Gregory XIII introduces the modern calendar.
1594	English navigator John Davis invents the backstaff.
1608	Dutch eyeglass-makers invent the first telescope.
1609	Galileo first uses the telescope for astronomy.
1618	Johannes Kepler discovers his first two laws of planetary motion.
1619	Kepler publishes his third law of planetary motion.
1687	Isaac Newton publishes the theory of universal gravitation and shows how the planets stay in orbit around the Sun.
1705	Edmond Halley predicts the return of Halley's Comet in 1758.

1770s	William Herschel begins building telescopes.	**1948**	George Gamow coins the term Big Bang theory.
1781	Herschel discovers the planet Uranus.	**1951–54**	Astronomers discover the spiral structure of our galaxy.
1800	Herschel discovers infrared radiation.	**1959**	First space probes are sent to the Moon.
1814	Joseph von Fraunhofer describes dark lines in the Sun's spectrum.	**1965**	Discovery of background radiation provides the first direct evidence of the Big Bang theory.
1846	Johann Galle discovers the planet Neptune.	**1961**	Thomas Matthews and Allan Sandage discover quasars using a radio telescope.
about 1859	Gustav Kirchhoff and Robert Bunsen first explain the dark lines in the Sun's spectrum.	**1972**	Satellite *Uhuru* scans the sky in the X-ray range and discovers Cygnus X-1.
1860–63	Astronomers first look at the spectra of stars.	**1977**	Discovery of rings around the planet Uranus.
1868	Pierre Janssen discovers a new element (helium) from studying the Sun's spectrum.	**1978**	Discovery of Pluto's moon, Charon.
1917	The 100-inch Hooker reflector telescope at Mount Wilson, California, is completed.	**1993**	Hubble Space Telescope sends back its first high-quality images.
1917	U.S. astronomer Harlow Shapley first suggests a structure for our galaxy.	**1999**	Chandra X-Ray Observatory is launched into orbit.
1922–24	Edwin Hubble proves that the galaxies lie beyond the Milky Way.	**2003**	Spitzer Space Telescope is launched into orbit.
1927	Hubble shows that the universe is expanding.	**2005**	NASA probe strikes Temple Comet.
1930s	Georges Lemaitre suggests that the universe may have begun in a huge explosion.	**2005**	Discovery of tenth planet.
1930	Clyde Tombaugh discovers Pluto.		
1937	First radio telescope is built.		

Glossary

astrology telling the future from the stars

atmosphere layer of air that surrounds Earth

black hole very tiny, very dense (heavy) object that has such strong gravity that not even light can escape from it

calendar way to keep track of time over days, months, and years

comet lump of ice and rock that travels in a huge orbit around the Sun

constellation pattern of stars

eclipse a solar eclipse happens when the Moon gets between Earth and the Sun. A lunar eclipse is when Earth's shadow falls on the Moon.

elements simplest materials, made of only a single kind of atom

elliptical oval-shaped

galaxy "island" of millions or billions of stars in space

gravity force between all objects that attracts them toward each other

infrared kind of radiation that has slightly less energy than visible light

latitude distance a place is north or south of the equator

lunar month time it takes the Moon to go from full to new (dark) and back again—about 29 days

matter "stuff" that everything in the universe is made of

Mesopotamia ancient kingdom in the Middle East, in what is now Iraq

meteor shower small pieces of rock and dust from space that burn up as they fall through the atmosphere

Middle Ages period of European history from about 450 to 1500

Milky Way our galaxy, the one that Earth and the Sun are part of

navigate to find your way around

nebula huge, bright cloud of gas and dust

optics study of light, lenses, and mirrors

orbit to go around

planet large object orbiting the Sun or another star

prism specially shaped piece of glass (usually pyramid-shaped) that is used to split light

quantum leap huge move forward

radiation light or other kinds of rays that are similar to light but invisible

reflecting telescope telescope that uses mirrors instead of lenses

satellite something that orbits Earth or another planet

solar year time taken for Earth to travel once around the Sun

spectrum (more than one are called spectra) range of colors formed when light is split using a prism

supernova huge explosion that happens when a very large star reaches the end of its life

Further Information

Books

Gow, Mary. *Tycho Brahe: Astronomer*. Berkeley Heights, N.J.: Enslow, 2002.

Graun, Ken, and Suzanne Maly. *Our Galaxy and the Universe*. Tucson, Ariz.: Ken Press, 2002.

Kerrod, Robin. *The Stars and Galaxies*. Chicago: Raintree, 2002.

Maestro, Betsy. *The Story of Clocks and Calendars*. New York: Lothrop, Lee & Shepard, 1999.

Mason, Paul. *Isaac Newton*. Chicago: Raintree, 2002.

Places to visit

Palomar Observatory
35899 Canfield Road
Palomar Mountain, Calif. 92060-0200
phone: (760) 742-2119

Mount Wilson Observatory
740 Holladay Road
Pasadena, Calif. 91106
phone: (626) 793-3100

Websites

Space and Beyond *http://kids.msfc.nasa.gov/Space/*
A website from NASA (the National Aeronautics and Space Administration) about Earth, the Moon, galaxies, and other space stuff. This site also includes the Astronomy Picture of the Day. Every day, this features an incredible picture from space and an explanation of what it is and who took the picture. There is an archive of pictures going back to 1995 and an index organized by subject.

Hubble Gallery *http://hubblesite.org/gallery/*
A gallery of pictures and movies from the Hubble Space Telescope.

Index